THE SALT
OF SOMETHING NEW

First published in 2026 by
The Dedalus Press
13 Moyclare Road
Baldoyle
Dublin D13 K1C2
Ireland

www.dedaluspress.com

ISBN 9781915629562 (hardback)
ISBN 9781915629579 (paperback)

Dedalus Press titles are available in Ireland
from Argosy Books (www.argosybooks.ie) and in the UK
from Inpress Books (www.inpressbooks.co.uk).
Printed in Dublin by Print Dynamics.

Cover artwork,
Where the Youghiogheny meets the Glennacally Bridge,
oils and vinyl emulsion on linen 110x80cm (2023),
by Caitlyn Rooke, by kind permission.
www.caitlynrooke.com

Dedalus Press receives financial assistance from
The Arts Council / An Chomhairle Ealaíon.

the arts council an chomhairle ealaíon funding literature

THE SALT
OF SOMETHING NEW

CHANDRIKA NARAYANAN-MOHAN

DEDALUS PRESS

Contents

I

II

III

to my family of storytellers

I

18.39 above Dublin

Hovering above the coast,
Dublin a shadow beyond the wing of a plane.
We are meandering, stalling, and it feels like

how I feel about home, waiting at the edge of things,
wondering when to enter, when to make
myself comfortable, how long to stay.

From this angle the water is a slab,
currents stretch-marking across its heave
with the oil-slick sheen of spoilt bacon.

Familiar cliffs cast shadows onto the sea.
For a moment the island seems to hover,
until a wind flicks the waves awake

along exposed beaches at low tide
where sand swirls and settles, reminiscent of fortunes
in Turkish coffee cups from another life.

I think about connections, commitments, islands,
what it means to stay, what it would feel like
to fly into an airport on a different coast

taking in a different shoreline,
taking on a different accent, but maybe
ready for the salt of something new.

Stargazing With My Mother

'We've seen stars fall before,' she texts

We peer out over rooftops
from different sides of Europe
looking for a blip or a spark against the blue
trying not to mistake a rocket for a star

'You need binoculars,' she says

I remember how she demonstrated
before handing me a pair
as the Hale-Bopp comet blazed across
a New Delhi sky

'Look, over there!' she exclaims

pointing to a needle streak of white
standing outside a Swiss hotel
not caring what people might think
of two Indian women gazing up into the night

Ararat

My mother is a Bible

she inks her sadness into uniform lines that I reach for
in the comfort of darkness, tracing fingers along familiar choices

My mother is a Prayer

she becomes the psalms I chew over dinner
the repetition in my fury, the snarl in my hair

My mother is Risen

she holds aloft a tumour, gold mosaic, the size of a cathedral
radiation like sunshine, warm with blood

My mother is a Prophecy

she screams across the desert, her tongue a testament
teetering above the memory of a deluge

Salthill and Monkstown

At Salthill and Monkstown
naked hipbones of sand
lie sleek in shallow water
deepening by Seapoint

there it is still
that wide curve of green
a path snaking upwards
towards stony walls

dark wooden pews
a hallway lit yellow
strangers in ill-fitting suits
and you, nowhere

The 10.35 from Belfast Central

a behemoth sweeps by in a screech of city-dust metal
warm blood on a cold spoon
Dublin wintersmell

a horror-movie clink of chains
is only the bulk of a man releasing his two-wheel steed
from a pole down the middle of O'Connell Street

I go north for the night
speeding around a different country
with voices like marbles in pinkfleshspit mouth

I return south in the morning
where in purple seats full of birdcage chatter
a woman praises Theresa May

her mouth closing around
the soft melt of a Cadbury's bar
I decline when she offers a piece

my phone has yet to alert me to
a change of provider and
the landscape betrays nothing—

only graveyards, silk-misted farmhouses
double-glazed windows sunk into brick
warming in the morning sun

Border Control

legging it off the plane to be first in line

striding through the airport queuing for hours
itchy feet until

blank-faced official

looks
types
doesn't smile
stamps

anxiety subsides

but today I am kissing the earth with speed
velvet hills whipping past in poison green
and bruised-lip blues
and the only sign of crossing
is a text on my screen

but my face gives away what my birthright lacks
so I keep hold of my passport
as we slip down the tracks

just in case the wind changes direction

Brexit Blues

it never really leaves you

in 2012 I cry in my bathrobe, I make a playlist
England I love you, but you're bringing me down
"the UK just dumped me"
my boyfriend doesn't get it

the country leaves my veins
I fall in love with a different river
with Dublin Bikes, 20-minute walks
I think, *I'd like to make you mine forever*

but it never really leaves you
four years later my heart is shredded anew
scared and anxious, reminding myself
that's not your home anymore

would I have the courage
to defeat a face-full of spit on a crowded street?
a slur like a cut across the eyeball?
would I be brave, would I intervene?

out of control, lashing out,
through centuries of sickness a country is set alight
the ugliness a shout behind a triumphant sneer
into the ear of terrified stranger

I thought I'd feel nothing
but it's bubbling black and viscous
I breathe relief on Irish soil
with my heart clenched like a fist

The First EU Passport I Ever Held Like It Was Mine

was found abandoned on a ledge

soaked, spine curved
opened to stained pages
a pale teenage face staring back
light wide eyes mouth slack
big ears on a buzzed head

slipped into my pocket
I touched the pages
a wrongness in the intimacy
of holding something so valuable
in its most weakened state

at Kevin Street station
I relinquish it to a Garda
the moment quickly over
pockets empty
grit on my fingertips

You City, You Boyfriend

Seated awkwardly on a wooden box
we're on the last of my cigarettes.
He talks, and talks, and my replies
are nothing but punctuation.
Under a brutalist tower, the city smirks,
raises an eyebrow as if to say,
'You know I'm better than him.'
And you're right.
When we converse, through the choke of soft air,
we exhale each other in whispers
on a walk home where a smile
has broken my face from the realisation that
yes, you are better than him.
You are better than all of them.
You push up through my soles and I feel every pebble
when I'm treading across your tar-bump skin.
I am embedded in you,
you city, you boyfriend, you dusty hug.
When I tell you you're beautiful, you blush across the canal
even though you already know that grey glamour suits you.
I wear you like an arm across my shoulder.
Like me, you play your cards close to your chest
but when we mourn we crack
with rain that pummels onto the pavements
and across a million cheap umbrellas.
So take me in and make me yours.
I've already let the pollen in my pores anoint me
to an orchestra of rustling leaves and seagull song,
and one day, I will take thee to be my lawful wedded home
and I shall wear a dress of summer fog

and a ring of past lives,
and you will smile, and shrug,
and in your humid indifference I will vow to love you anyway
because I'm a hopeless romantic,
and you're a city that keeps its own name.

Missing Bin Day

Scrolling through NASA's Instagram to get over you
        a mass of bodies writhing on the surface of Jupiter
                        as the soap you left behind runs out
the universe gives a wink   I drop the last sliver down the drain

the bathroom bin still houses your used condoms
the one in the kitchen, a mess of   *bananaeggshellpotatopeel*
        a cauldron fermenting and ripening, begging to be
bagged,   tagged,   discarded on the pavement
                            picked to pieces by a passing gull

Cured

Summer leaves me hanging off hooks
a freshly butchered pig
fat sizzling in the heat.

It is not the season of fruit bearing
of buxom sweetness that gives, fulfils, nourishes
composts at the end of the garden.

Instead I ferment, meat-slick, citrus-slimed
black around the edges, fuzzy with parasites
aged, cleaned, consumed.

İskender Kebap

My mother's grief chokes her to the gullet, stuffs
her full with the thick meat of loss, each death
another slab on the skewer: pets, exes, parents,
tightly compressed, the juice of them flowing
clear, cooking slowly, rotating, scraping away
at her insides. I want to open the oven of
her ribs, reach in, let the heat out, shave
the tower down for her strip by greasy
strip, lift each piece, count the layers
like rings of a tree. I want to place
her grief onto warm *pide*
drizzled with *domatesli*
sos and sizzling butter,
with a side of fresh
yoğurt, garnished
with a single *biber.*
I want to present
it to her on a
plate, which
she will push
away. *Eat it,*
Mum, just
fucking
eat.

Bog Body

tension sings across the night
pulls at the peat in my veins towards
the mulch and dirt rolling off you
pouring out your mouth

I wish it could cover
my eyes my nostrils
it's the only way
to love you

the way grit presses into pores
the way giants roam your dreams
the way roots
wrap around a corpse

I long to engulf you
in the warm wet earth
where some stories end
and others begin

Viola

where dishwater clouds met a roiling sea
I thought I saw you
in the swoop of a gull
in the beat of the wind
in the window of a neighbouring house
dark polished wood in hand
greasy where your chin rested
bow freshly frayed where your fingers
pushed and plucked and tore to ribbons

Superglue

Another chip from a favourite bowl
pressed back into place
relish the nestle of it
the perfect rupture

along the bottom   a faultline
trace it shining like a trail of spittle
the vacuum's cheap plastic cracks
another thing to fix   drip drip   hold in place

when glue coats your fingers
wait
let it harden
chew the last of your skin off
spit it into the sink

Stoppered

reeking of bonfire
winedrizzled
hotmouthed
thinking of a girl
I once wanted
to make my wife
but what good
am I across a sea
drunk and
full of silence

Ride

i. Meringue

your face creases when you
smile / freshly whipped /
I could lick the spoon
of ye / till the bowl
shines clean

ii. Candy Crush

rain hits the roof
crackle and fizz
popping candy
open your mouth
let it sizzle
swallow hard

iii. First Time

missed the last bus
we shrug
raise eyebrows
my wine-stung mouth
your weed-sweet tongue

iv. Plasticine

pressing into you
until you can feel
my fingerprints on
the back of your neck

v. Not Forever, It Turns Out

the door shut downstairs
trail of departure smoking
on musty carpet
I still haven't moved
toothpaste mint sting tingle
fading from my lips

vi. Evening on North Frederick Street

I've seen this colour before
in boxes of broken crayons
was it Prussian blue?
now melted wax across the sky
a velvet backdrop to my home
where you are inside
saying your goodbyes

vii. Eyeliner

a deep sable knife strike against an eyelid
my hand paused precariously
painting over exhaustion
trapping each bead of grief
under black tarmac

viii. Solstice

I hope we meet again
where light stretches over the bones of night
and the thin skin of day
drapes over the tops of trees

ix. Solo

a holy quiet
in the church of my ribs
warm light overhead
soft rug underfoot
soothed by the buzz
of a small fridge
drinking from the font
of my own solitude

When we meet (I'll take you to Armagh)

where

gold-leafed constellations

dot polished granite

where

the wanderings of a solar system

mark the ground

I'll take you to the gift shop

buy you an umbrella

flimsy

silver

covered in stars

II

A moment please to unlace myself while I

take a soft toothbrush
blessed with plaque

scrub at the muck
the brown and the gunk

watch it slide off leather and Gore-Tex
watch the bristles loosen mud

remove a memory of bonesoak and gust
of wet straw and murky slurp

wipe away the hum and whistle
watch grit swirl in the sink

resist the urge to scoop it up
stuff it into my mouth

Hike

touching bog wood
wet, blood-red, femur-bent
looking like anger ossified

river-sucked and wind-torn
I grabbed at straw
wrapped it around a fist

a foothold
an anchor
a leash

The Knee

after Jane Hirshfield

The knee is not a city
of hollow cathedrals and patella gates,
of stitched ligament and stretched muscle,
the empty agora where blood once
gathered, then evacuated.

It is not the Velcro crunch of itself
as it bends and carries,
the ache and the strain,
the burden of movement.

It is not even a nudge into
the crook of your bent leg,
the puzzle piece of it,
where it whispers to your tendons
in the night.

It is not a rock face,
pock-marked, water-carved
allowing itself to be hollowed,
lived in, river-rushed.

Only in rest is it a mountain range,
silent and busy under a dark sky,
allowing safe passage
through a burdenless night.

Midnight at Busáras

The No. 32 from Letterkenny pulls in. Yawning passengers clamber gracelessly down, haul suitcases, loop plastic bags over aching shoulders.

Underground, sconces flicker. Broken chairs once freshly velvet creak and shift. A newsreel threads itself through a projector, lighting the screen in twilight hues.

At the top of the building, mosaic shimmers from the walls, peeking out from the underside of a covered balcony. Stones stretch across abandoned spaces.

Downstairs they wait for taxis, backs to it all.

The Cats of St Catherine's

The cats of St Catherine's
promenade along garage roofs
across work-from-home shed/offices
along the corrugated
the tiled
the bricked
the tarmacked
See the shape of them ebb and flow as they
congregate
confer

silently part ways
white socks flashing against the dark

Nightboarder

In the silent nightwet neighbourhood
a boy skateboards in the rain
wheels protesting against the pavement

passing under my window
he crescendoes like a fighter jet
a roar echoing off lightshut houses

when he turns the corner
the night ruffles its feathers, settles
until only the sound of rain remains

Run

i.m. Aisling Murphy

nightwalk, moonbright, wet leaf smell
rustling bushes, cans in the canal

manlit, moonlit, or daylit
all the places we can't go for fear of
pain or rape or a throat slit
a body in a bush, newflash, press pit
what-was-she-wearings and asking-for-its

sprouting leaves, bristles form
sweet green shoots, purple thorn

loud parties with groping male friends
no one pushes them off, stems
the flow of attention, the persistence of men,
the approaching shadows, the 'text-me-whens'

lavender stalk between thumb and forefinger
lamplit winternight, neighbourhood linger

towpath bogeymen, park attack
the levy breaks and bloats and cracks
assault stats well up and flood their banks
unsavoury girls live in charts and graphs
not in the Tesco newspaper stacks

reed-hushed swans and dirt-path ghosts
keen by rivers, brooks and coasts
rattled fathers after morning runs
pause when looking at their sons

Wuthering Heights

I am seeing the bog as if it were the moor
the trappings of it, a gale that presses you in place
the treachery in the space between two houses

ligaments straining in the language of escape
the suck of soil underfoot
traversing it strapped to screaming life

sick with terror and fury
shattered and sodden
until finally
a road

Downwind of Sally's Bridge

I've never sat on the banks of the canal
alone in the dark
back to the path
oblivious to danger
to people who might take a notion
and push me in

but wedged between the water
the bushes the mud the bricks
a girl sits serenely

I wonder if she breathes easy
as I walk by along the path
nerves fizzing on her behalf

Oracle

Based on an interview with Met Éireann meteorologist Linda Hughes

Girls aren't supposed to play with storms but I am wound around them, their intricacies, soft breezes and brutalities. Why wouldn't this be a place for a girl? Surely we belong in the eye of things, in the precision point of potential destruction, haven't we always been seer, soothsayer, truthteller, Cassandra? Eyes always on things that shift, that flow, that rise and fall, the patterns of the world. Mouthpiece for foretelling, numbers and statistics flowing from fingertips, all lipstick and research. I hope they see me, messy pigtails, diamond-eyed, lightning-brained, I hope they point at the screen and ready themselves, curiosity ignited, prepared to step into a world of wind and blaze, salted equations, dark water and sky.

The girl ~~and~~ is the tower

Based on an interview with instrument scientist Dr Temilade Adegoke

the girl is the tower is the little Lego man is the girl
staring at the screen, legs tired, boots chafing
until the images of nanowires are burnt into her eyeballs
stamped onto her corneas
her favourite film projected on repeat
onto the back of her skull

at home in bed when she closes her eyes
flaky tendrils and blurry grids
pulse with promise and power
and when she has nightmares
they are of dendrites and
exploding batteries and cars on fire
of dragging the carcass of hope
back to square one, the smell of
burning is still in her hair when she wakes

but now when she dreams
on the occasional night of solid sleep
soft smile, warm pillow, furrowed brow
she dreams of the perfect day
when the sample prep is successful and her eyes
light up, everything aligns just right

let's not think of replicating this perfection
not now, let her enjoy the moment
when it's just her and the screen
the girl and the microscope the size of a room

they are Gemini souls, woman and microscope
let them blaze quietly together

In the museum,

Paula Rego is wrestling with the universe, with what a story/
a woman/time can look like in 1962, in bulbous colour and chaos.

In the next room Fernanda Fragateiro constructs wooden
beams, comforting scaffolding: *here, I made this for you, look how
simple it can be? It's hard and has edges.*

Around the corner, Adriana Varejão knows the world is
pulsating meat and organ under white and blue tiles.

Upstairs, the boys, *brâncusimanraypicassowarholdalí*
do what they usually do (maybe that's reductive).

In the bowels of the building, the women's meaty presence
summons craving, envy, makes words anaemic, clumsy,

fleshandmeatandwoodandpaintandandpaperandsinewand

Emmy Noether

German Jewish mathematician (1882–1935), described by Albert Einstein and others as 'the most important woman in the history of mathematics.'

Famous for flagrant gesticulation
her tumble of hairpins a cascade of enthusiasm
the crumb and the stain and the mess of her dress
that appalled and offended
those cleaner and neater

the symphony she conducted
ideas plaited around wild fingers
loosed onto seeking minds
gathered in her home
when banned everywhere else

the whirr of a bicycle wheel
how it stays true in its rickety clatter
her postcards crammed with formulae and chatter
spitting sparks and setting alight
until the world of maths caught ablaze

equations threading through her veins
tumbling out her mouth at speed
a universe falls into place in her name
through planets, stars,
the orbits of moons

despite those who craved her silence
the universe continues to unfurl
in the grip of her equations
a symphony continuing
in her absence

Perseverance

Inspired by the Mars Perseverance rover press conference

i. Gyroscope

camera attached
ready for launch
a girl stands
her father in attendance
to bear witness

she reaches skywards
    then tilts
        bends
            is for a split second
        weightless
    as her legs whip over
ending in a gymnast's triumphant stance

her father
for a moment
    imagines whorls of red dust
    swirling around her
her firmly planted feet

ii. Hearing Mars

over a tinny whine
a girl hears the rustle-thud
of the Martian air, the dry red gust of it
she listens intently to an alien wind
and feels at home

Scallop

Based on an interview with marine bioscientist Dr Siddhi Joshi

It starts with Blue Planet
the gentle voice, sweeping shots,
dart flick and shimmer.

Curiosity becomes intention becomes
an ocean crossed, becomes map, becomes
sonar and seabed and eager eyes.

An ocean crossed again, back on an island
where the lure of drills and rigs and viscous gold
make the air thick with unbelonging.

This time it doesn't take an ocean.
A narrow sea brings me to sediment and maerl,
to watery beings, to salt-flecked kin.

Off a Galway shore, amongst red algae,
the shimmerlilac of a coraline maze,
a heartbeat calms and slows, safe at last.

III

'Life is really good'

he says, no longer the lanky teenager under colourful lights,
feral with hope and fear and heartbreak. His edges now
rounded, he seems cared for, openly loved, electric with purpose.

He sighs, relaxed and slightly drunk, weaves tales for the room
with elegant hands that sweep the summer evening air,
scooping our bated breaths like snowballs.

After an applause he offers his hand, his open palm a blooming
lotus. I accept it awkwardly, like a handshake, easing into the
unfamiliar comfort of friendship.

I press my hand into his, wishing for osmosis, willing his ease
into my pores. But there is only the dampness of a brotherly
hand, and something like love.

for Stephen Clare

Editor

for a friend

I am editing your poem
the one you've emailed from the psychiatric ward
you say the indentations are wrong because
of the formatting on your phone

I am texting you edits
'stanza 1, line 2: do you need this hyphen?'
I don't ask how you are or why you are there
all that matters is that

you've sent me a poem

perhaps it contains all the answers
to the questions inside me
about a place where I once thought
might be right for me

Instead I tell you to
write 'then' instead of 'than'
to trim the fat, to keep going
because you're doing so well

Eithne Takes the Form of a Raven

for Eithne Casey and the Song House Poets

Eithne dances, and we watch
the fluorescent lights flash off

the silver spikes studding her
discount Arnott's brogues,

her heels cracking whipsharp
against the wooden floor in

time with Ruben's bodhrán and
Andrew's whistlefluting,

the clink of Mary's wedding ring against
her wine glass, percussing keenly,

glinting like the constellation
that rings the blue of Eithne's eyes.

Lupin Seeds

I want to bring her with me
unable to lift the bubbling stream
reluctant to snip wide palms of mint

a tower of lupin pods, seeds
brown and cracking, tiny offerings
to be buried in new dirt

seven embryos in a pod
the whole tower rattles
when I pull it away

back inside I notice
a caterpillar on my shoulder
I shake it off, apologising

the garden makes its own rules
about what can be taken
and who can leave

River Mill

for Paul Maddern

I find two knobbly apples on the grass
a worm wriggles out
disappears with the flick of a finger

I bring them into the kitchen
he eyes them warily but thanks me,
accepting with a nod

when he turns back to the oven
he is a swaying stalk
of flowering mint

a blink of montbretia
a tangle of succulents
the memory of a fallen willow tree

Sea

You are the soft-warm
blood-calm
the splot and the lick
the wet-mouth pulse
the salty freeze
the seizure, the cradling
the deep-light hold of you
pale sun glimmer, glass-shard
ferocity of you

I have never been held by
this many hands before
so much seething
ice-veined life in you

sink me, drag me below
your horizon-line honesty
the love and the death
the salt fleck, white foam
retreating gulp of you
that spits me back out
hungry, restless

soil-sick

winterswim

fragments of lake
crumple around the shower drain
rock and slimy grassblade

memory of needleskin and freeze
knifebite and shriekthrill
melts under hot water

I melt with it, blood and tumble
fleshtingle, muscleripple
I come so fast, laugh so loud

Annaghmakerrig

Sidestepping pine cones
engraved faces upturned
small nutty rosebuds
wound tight and round

above, a gasping abundance
endless branches laden with cones
they pock and thread against the sky
wintry explosion of spiral and ball

a kite shrieks and trills from beyond
a triumph of things once lost returning
a harbinger of resurrections
singing to a cornucopia of seeds

Balscadden Beach

She offered me the sea.
The first time in the swift blink of summer
when my own home was a fist.

Gifted a sanctuary by the water,
a vast sparkling seduction by day,
by night an endless obsidian tongue.

Sleeping with the window open,
the roar and hush a salve
to impatient footsteps on wooden floors.

First time swimming alone,
I'm staring the horizon in the eye
its kindly cold freeze holding me firm.

In time I built my own sanctuary
above pavements, buses, rooftops,
a soft, small room gazing into the sky.

This time when she offered me the sea,
the grey diamond swell, the whistling wind,
I chose land.

Our Lady of Dublin

I pledge my fidelity to you, and only you
There is no republic that can contain me
Like you I am languid, ruthless, mercurial

I vow to uphold the values of a flowing river
I pledge my allegiance to cracked concrete
I will tend to precious havens of holy soil

I have burned and blistered and raged
And have forsaken those charred restraints
As I submit the rawness of myself to your waters

Let my hopes echo through your mountains
Let my dreams be sown deep
Let my roots sink to the wet below

Aflame and submerged
Torn and reborn
The salt of you upon my tongue

I continue to rise, with you

a Pledge of Citizenship 19.12.2023

Clear History

'What isn't meant for you
will pass you by' she says
the houses I once wanted
no more than 404s
in my browser history

like deleted screenshots
blocked contacts
search results for
engagement rings
cache-cleared

long forgotten

Thaw

i.

I don't make a habit of marvelling men
but when you're shower-fresh at the breakfast table
I stare like I summoned you out of dust motes
surprised when the shape of you actually appeared

ii.

The day you moved in, the daffodils bloomed
nodding their frilled heads towards the moving van
the lawn grew its first daisy, a singular sprig of white
against sunbursted green

iii.

Potting tomatoes
shaking seedlings loose
we work in easy silence
sun kissing things that grow

Oscar Square Birthday Party

In the aftermath of a wintry spring
cherry blossom confetti lines the streets
tucked into the cracks of gutters
skitters across roads, under passing cars

Children have gone home
the streets have a cutlery-clink dinnertime hush
with air that smells like spuds on a roasting tray
I breathe in the burn and cook of it

A bloom of dark clouds begins to gather
bleeding into a Victoria sponge sunset
a cake-scented breeze teases past
whispering, 'make a wish'

Summer Songs

her voice sweet and ragged
a woman sings
I hear her through one ear
the other pressed against your cheek
until it suctions to you
until I hear the factory roar of blood
the distant chime of your heart
the click and grind of jaw
the squirrelly sound as you swallow
while the orchestra of your body
accompanies her into the final verse
you unfold yourself
your spine reaching upwards
I unlock from you with a pop
barely audible against the applause

Open Windows

The kitchen smells like American brownies
a Betty-Crocker-fudge-crackle-topped traybake kind of good

From outside the scent of wet ground,
like monsoon porches, Delhi city rain

The bedroom heavy with jasmine oil, like
stolen flowers from Phibsborough, night-fresh and white-bright

A Dublin apartment, smelling like
family, memories, loneliness, homes.

86 Trees

I could get used to south-westerly sun
hot tea cooling in the wind
a book perched on a leg
the squall and flutter of birds
hopping and swelling

I count the trees from my position
behind an uncollected skip
I start and stop 3 times, lose count
get to 86, marvel at it

watch dandelions sprout
between the cracks of a driveway
my driveway
on this catless street
wings reign supreme

amongst the leaves
yours yours yours
and across the threshold
mine mine mine

Imbolg

I am on the way to love
sunset-kissed and cloud-hugged
passport-laden, belted up
sister-bound and soulmate-stretched

a baking soda vinegar volcano
its fizz and roar scrubbing away
the empty years, hollow days
                    and the—

          we won't talk about that now
          not under a violet sky
          not under an Imbolg moon
          winter has ended
                    and I am on my way to love

ACKNOWLEDGEMENTS & THANKS

The author wishes to express her thanks to the publishers and editors of the following in which a number of these poems, or versions of them, originally appeared:

Flare: Readings from the Sunflower Sessions, Green Carnations, Glas na Gile: 25 Young LGBTQ+ Poets from Ireland (Book Hub Publishing), *Honest Ulsterman, I Am the Wind: Irish Poems for Children Everywhere* (Little Island), *Impossible Archetype, Local Wonders: Poems of Our Immediate Surrounds* (Dedalus Press), *Queering the Green: Post-2000 Queer Irish Poetry* (Lifeboat Press), *The Stinging Fly, This Is What You Mean To Me: Poetry Ireland Introductions 2021* (Poetry Ireland), *Writing Home: the 'New Irish' Poets* (Dedalus Press). Also thank you to the Irish Writers Centre and the Institute of Physics for commissioning poems in this collection.

*

Every poem here can be traced back to open mic nights, workshops, festivals, retreats, residencies, theatre shows, writing groups, text messages, group chats, video calls, and hangouts. Poetry is communal and all the more wonderful for it.

Thank you to Anne Tannam for your friendship and for mentoring me on this manuscript; to Annemarie Ní Churreáin for the poems written during your Song House retreat; to the Tyrone Guthrie Centre at Annaghmakerrig; to Paul Maddern at the River Mill and your lemon meringue pie; to the Poetry Ireland Introductions 2021 crew; to the Irish Writers Centre; to Angela Carr, your monthly submission list helped me get my poems out into the world; to the Arts Council of Ireland for Agility and Project Awards; to the Science Gallery Dublin team who were the first to support my science poems; to Brendan Owens and the Institute of Physics for making me their writer in residence, leading to the creation of those physicist poems; to the Skein Beans for pointing me in the right direction; to Caitlyn Rooke for allowing the use of her beautiful painting as the book cover; to my readers Adelle Hay, Polina Cosgrave, Rafael Mendes, and Tiny Bae a.k.a Eva O'Connor; to everyone who inspired poems, from beautiful friends to former partners; to Aodh O'Sullivan for being the maerl to my scallop; to Melissa Clissold for your support, friendship, and sisterhood, and for telling me I was always going to write a book.

Although Ireland made me a writer, much of this journey started long before moving here. Thank you to my family for being the art lovers that made me a reader and a writer. Thank you especially to my wonderful mother, for inspiring some of my best poems and for genetically gifting me both creative writing skills and great skin, and for teaching me that art and science have always gone hand in hand. Thank you to my high school English teachers Shannon Westgate and Jo-Anne Ahlmén for your encouragement and enthusiasm.

Finally thank you to Pat Boran and Chiamaka Enyi-Amadi for publishing me for the first time in October 2019 in *Writing Home,* setting many of us migrant writers on the path we're now on. You took many chances on me, Pat, this book was meant to happen with you.